300 words

Level 1

审石头

A Stone on Trial

宋晶 改编 吴爱俊 翻译

MP3

Download Online

SinolinguA

华语教学出版社

First Edition 2018

ISBN 978-7-5138-1478-2

Published by Sinolingua Co., Ltd
24 Baiwanzhuang Road, Beijing 100037, China
Tel: (86) 10-68320585 68997826
Fax: (86) 10-68997826 68326333
http://www.sinolingua.com.cn
E-mail: hyjx@sinolingua.com.cn
Facebook: www.facebook.com/sinolingua
Printed by Beijing Jinghua Hucais Printing Co., Ltd

Printed in the People's Republic of China

编者的话

对于广大汉语学习者来说，要想快速提高汉语水平，扩大阅读量是很有必要的。“彩虹桥”汉语分级读物为汉语学习者提供了一系列有趣、有用的汉语阅读材料。本系列读物按照词汇量进行分级，力求用限定的词汇讲述精彩的故事。本套读物主要有以下特点：

一、分级精准，循序渐进。我们参考“新汉语水平考试（HSK）词汇表”（2012 年修订版）、《汉语国际教育用音节汉字词汇等级划分（国家标准）》和《常用汉语 1500 高频词语表》等词汇分级标准，结合《欧洲语言教学与评估框架性共同标准》（CEFR），设计了一套适合汉语学习者的“彩虹桥”词汇分级标准。本系列读物分为 7 个级别（入门级 *、1 级、2 级、3 级、4 级、5 级、6 级），供不同水平的汉语学习者选择，每个级别故事的生词数量不超过本级别对应词汇量的 20%。随着级别的升高，故事的篇幅逐渐加长。本系列读物与 HSK、CEFR 的对应级别，各级词汇量以及每本书的字数详见下表。

* 入门级（Starter）在封底用 S 标识。

级别	入门级	1 级	2 级	3 级	4 级	5 级	6 级
对应级别	HSK1 CEFR A1	HSK1-2 CEFR A1-A2	HSK2-3 CEFR A2-B1	HSK3 CEFR A2-B1	HSK3-4 CEFR B1	HSK4 CEFR B1-B2	HSK5 CEFR B2-C1
词汇量	150	300	500	750	1 000	1 500	2 500
字数	1 000	2 500	5 000	7 500	10 000	15 000	25 000

二、故事精彩，题材多样。本套读物选材的标准就是“精彩”，所选的故事要么曲折离奇，要么感人至深，对读者构成奇妙的吸引力。选题广泛取材于中国的神话传说、民间故事、文学名著、名人传记和历史故事等，让汉语学习者在阅读中潜移默化地了解中国的文化和历史。

三、结构合理，实用性强。“彩虹桥”系列读物的每一本书中，除了中文故事正文之外，都配有主要人物的中英文介绍、生词英文注释及例句、故事正文的英文翻译、练习题和生词表，方便读者阅读和理解故事内容，提升汉语阅读能力。练习题主要采用客观题，题型多样，难度适中，并附有参考答案，既可供汉语教师在课堂上教学使用，又可供汉语学习者进行自我水平检测。

如果您对本系列读物有什么想法，比如推荐精彩故事、提出改进意见等，请发邮件到 liuxiaolin@sinolingua.com.cn，与我们交流探讨。也可以关注我们的微信公众号 CHQRainbowBridge，随时与我们交流互动。同时，微信公众号会不定期发布有关“彩虹桥”的出版信息，以及汉语阅读、中国文化小知识等。

韩　颖　刘小琳

Preface

For students who study Chinese as a foreign language, it's crucial for them to enlarge the scope of their reading to improve their comprehension skills. The "Rainbow Bridge" Graded Chinese Reader series is designed to provide a collection of interesting and useful Chinese reading materials. This series grades each volume by its vocabulary level and brings the learners into every scene through vivid storytelling. The series has the following features:

I. A gradual approach by grading the volumes based on vocabulary levels. We have consulted the New HSK Vocabulary (2012 Revised Edition), the *Graded Chinese Syllables, Characters and Words for the Application of Teaching Chinese to the Speakers of Other Languages (National Standard)* and the 1,500 Commonly Used High Frequency Chinese Vocabulary, along with the Common European Framework of Reference for Languages (CEFR) to design the "Rainbow Bridge" vocabulary grading standard. The series is divided into seven levels (Starter*, Level 1, Level 2, Level 3, Level 4, Level 5 and Level 6) for students at different stages in their Chinese education to choose from. For each level, new words are no more than 20% of the vocabulary amount as specified in the corresponding HSK and CEFR levels. As the levels progress, the passage length will in turn increase. The following table indicates the corresponding "Rainbow Bridge" level, HSK and CEFR levels, the vocabulary amount, and number of characters.

* Represented by "S" on the back cover.

Level	Starter	1	2	3	4	5	6
HSK/ CEFR Level	HSK1 CEFR A1	HSK1-2 CEFR A1-A2	HSK2-3 CEFR A2-B1	HSK3 CEFR A2-B1	HSK3-4 CEFR B1	HSK4 CEFR B1-B2	HSK5 CEFR B2-C1
Vocabulary	150	300	500	750	1,000	1,500	2,500
Characters	1,000	2,500	5,000	7,500	10,000	15,000	25,000

II. Intriguing stories on various themes. The series features engaging stories known for their twists and turns as well as deeply touching plots. The readers will find it a joyful experience to read the stories. The topics are selected from Chinese mythology, legends, folklore, literary classics, biographies of renowned people and historical tales. Such wide-ranging topics exert an invisible, yet formative, influence on readers' understanding of Chinese culture and history.

III. Reasonably structured and easy to use. For each volume of the "Rainbow Bridge" series, apart from a Chinese story, we also provide an introduction to the main characters in Chinese and English, new words with English explanations and sample sentences, and an English translation of the story, followed by comprehension exercises and a vocabulary list to help users read and understand the story and improve their Chinese reading skills. The exercises are mainly presented as objective questions that take on various forms with moderate difficulty. Moreover, keys to the exercises are also provided. The series can be used by teachers in class or by students for self-study.

If you have any questions, comments or suggestions about the series, please email us at liuxiaolin@sinolingua.com.cn. You can also exchange ideas with us via our WeChat account: CHQRainbowBridge. This account will provide updates on the series along with Chinese reading materials and cultural tips.

Han Ying and Liu Xiaolin

中文故事

① 审 (shěn) *v.*
try, interrogate
e.g., 法官审案一定要公正。

② 石头 (shítou) *n.*
stone
e.g., 把这块石头搬走吧，放在这里妨碍交通。

③ 纸 (zhǐ) *n.* paper
e.g., 你可以在这张纸上画画儿。

④ 价格 (jiàgé) *n.* price
e.g., 这件衣服的价格有点儿高。

⑤ 划船 (huá chuán) *v.*
row (a boat)
e.g., 春天来了，我们去公园划船吧。

⑥ 停 (tíng) *v.* park, berth
e.g., 学校门口不可以停车。

⑦ 河 (hé) *n.* river
e.g., 这条小河的水可真清呀！

⑧ 火把 (huǒbǎ) *n.*
torch
e.g., 晚上，山里的人用火把照明。

⑨ 刀 (dāo) *n.*
knife, sword
e.g., 上飞机不可以带刀。

审①石头②

很多年前，有个人叫一相（Yīxiàng），他是江西（Jiāngxī）人。因为广州（Guǎngzhōu）的纸③价格④很高，他就划着船⑤到广州去卖纸。这天晚上，他把船停⑥在河⑦边，就住在船上。在他快要睡着的时候，很多人拿着火把⑧和大刀⑨，跑到船

上抢[1]走了他的纸。一相非常害怕[2]，就躲[3]了起来，才没有被发现。第二天早上，他跑去官府[4]里报了案[5]。

这个地方的官员姓郭(Guō)，是个很聪明[6]的人。一相对他说："老爷[7]，我从江西划船来这里卖纸。可是，昨天晚上有很多坏人跑到我的船上，把我的纸都抢走

① 抢 (qiǎng) *v.* rob, loot, scramble for
e.g., 那个男人抢走了她的钱包。

② 害怕 (hàipà) *adj.* scared, frightened
e.g., 天黑了，我一个人在家很害怕。

③ 躲 (duǒ) *v.* hide
e.g., 小男孩儿躲到了门后面。

④ 官府 (guānfǔ) *n.* administrative body
e.g., 这是一座古代的官府。

⑤ 报案 (bào àn) *v.* report a case
e.g., 我的手机丢了，我要赶紧去报案。

⑥ 聪明 (cōngmíng) *adj.* smart, intelligent
e.g., 他是个聪明的小孩儿。

⑦ 老爷 (lǎoye) *n.* lord, master
e.g., 郭老爷办案很认真。

① 清楚 (qīngchu)
adj. clear
e.g., 你坐在后面能不能看清楚黑板?

了！请您帮帮我，把我的纸找回来吧！”

郭老爷问道：“你看清楚①那些坏人的样子了吗？”

“天太黑了，我没有看清楚。”一相说。

“那我怎么帮你找？这太难了！”

一相听了很着急：“老爷，您一定要帮帮我

啊，买纸的钱都是我借来的，如果找不回纸，我就没办法[1]回家了！这可怎么办啊？”

郭老爷听了，说：“你先不要急，我再想想办法。”

怎么样才能抓[2]到抢纸的坏人呢？郭老爷想了又想，有了一个好办法。他马上找来四个差人[3]，让他

① 办法 (bànfǎ) *n.*
method, solution
e.g., 你有什么好办法吗？

② 抓 (zhuā) *v.*
capture
e.g., 警察们下定决心，一定要抓到杀人犯。

③ 差人 (chāirén) *n.*
bailiff, runner
e.g., 差人负责完成官员交给他们的工作。

① 带 (dài) *v.* take, bring
e.g., 上课的时候可别忘了带书。

们去看看哪里有人在卖纸。

四个差人刚来到城门外，就看见一个人在路边卖纸。差人们带①着这个人回来见郭老爷。

郭老爷问卖纸的人：“你叫什么名字？”

那人说：“我叫胡桂(Hú Guì)。”

郭老爷又对差人说：“去叫一相来看看，胡桂卖的是不是他的纸。”

不一会儿，一相就来了。郭老爷问：“一相，这是你的纸吗？”

一相认真地看了又看，说：“是的！这就是我的纸！我卖的纸，左下角都有一个小小的‘相’字。你们看，这些纸每一张上都有这个‘相’字！”

① 腿 (tuǐ) *n.* leg
e.g., 我的腿有点儿疼。

郭老爷生气地问胡桂："你为什么要抢别人的纸？"

胡桂着急了，忙说："老爷，我没有抢他的纸呀！我的家里只有一个老母亲，我的腿①又不好，走路都很难，怎么可能去抢别人的东西呢？"

郭老爷听他说得也没

错，就又问："那么，你卖的纸是从哪里来的？快快说明白！"

胡桂说："今天早上，我去河边打水，看到河边的地上有很多纸，就把它们拿回了家。我妈妈对我说，你可以把纸拿出去卖呀，再买点儿吃的回来，咱们有好几天都没吃饱[1]了。可是，老爷，我真不知道这些纸是从

① 饱 (bǎo) *adj.* full, replete
e.g., 我吃饱了，你再吃一点儿。

哪里来的呀！”

郭老爷听了，点点头，说：“好吧，我不知道你说的是不是真的。差人们，先把胡桂关起来，等抓到了真正的坏人，再让他回去。”

胡桂听了，哭了起来，说：“老爷，把我关起来没什么，可我家里就只有我的老母亲一个人了，她可怎么办啊！”

郭老爷听了他的话，笑了，说：“你倒是很孝顺[1]，这么孝顺的人应该不会去做坏事。那你先回去吧！如果纸是你抢的，我一定不会放过你！”

胡桂走了。郭老爷想：“如何才能抓到那些坏人呢？”他问一相：“你停船的地方有什么东西吗？”

① 孝顺 (xiàoshùn) *v.* show filial piety
e.g., 他妈妈在病床上躺了三年，他很孝顺，一直照顾妈妈。

一相想了想，说：“河边有一块大石头。”

郭老爷认真地说：“这个石头一定知道谁抢了你的纸。”然后，他大声说：“来人！去河边把石头给我带回来，我要好好问问它，看是谁抢走了一相的纸！”

说完，他就找来十几个差人，去河边把那块大石头抬①了回来。

差人们把石头放在大厅②中间，郭老爷一本正经③地审问："石头，你快说，到底是谁抢走了一相的纸？"

差人们都偷偷④地笑了，说："老爷是在开玩笑吗？石头怎么会说话呀？"

很快，人们就都知道了郭老爷审石头的事情。大家很好奇⑤，都跑来看郭老爷怎么让石头"说话"。郭老爷看到有这么多人来，就让差人打开了官府的大门，让大家都进来。

郭老爷认真地问石头："石头，一相的纸被人抢

① 抬 (tái) *v.* carry, move
e.g., 我们两个人才能抬起这张桌子。

② 大厅 (dàtīng) *n.* hall
e.g., 我们明早在大厅见面。

③ 一本正经 (yìběn-zhèngjīng) in all seriousness
e.g., 看着三岁的孩子一本正经地读书的样子，我笑出了声。

④ 偷偷 (tōutōu) *adv.* stealthily, on the sly
e.g., 姥姥偷偷地给我带了好吃的。

⑤ 好奇 (hàoqí) *adj.* curious
e.g., 我很好奇这个盒子里装的是什么。

了，你一定知道是谁抢的，快点儿说出来！”郭老爷问了三次，但是，石头却什么都没说。

郭老爷很生气，大叫：“来人，你们重打石头二十下，看它说不说！”

人们看见了，都大笑起来。

郭老爷生气地说：“你们笑什么？来人！把大门关上，谁都不可以出去！”大门被关上了，刚才还在大笑的人们现在都有点儿害怕。

郭老爷问大家：“你们敢[1]在这里笑我，也太不把我放在眼里了！你们是愿

① 敢 (gǎn) *v.* dare
e.g., 我不敢一个人去那么远的地方。

意交①罚金②呢，还是愿意挨打③？”

人们都说：“我们愿意交罚金。”

郭老爷听了，说：“那好，你们把名字、家里的地址④都写下来，我可以让你们先回去。但你们每个人要交一百张纸来，当是

① 交 (jiāo) *v.* hand over, submit
e.g., 你交作业了吗？

② 罚金 (fájīn) *n.* fine, forfeit
e.g., 他交了罚金之后被放了出来。

③ 挨打 (ái dǎ) suffer from beating
e.g., 这个小孩儿很可怜，在家里经常挨打。

④ 地址 (dìzhǐ) *n.* address
e.g., 我知道他家的地址，我带你去。

罚金。”人们听了，虽然都很不高兴，但是也没有办法，只好写下名字和地址，回家准备纸去了。

这天下午，大家都回到官府里，把准备好的纸交了上来。人们交纸的时候，郭老爷让一相就在旁

① 比较 (bǐjiào) *v.* compare
e.g., 我比较了一下两种水果的价格，决定还是买便宜的。

边看着，看这里有没有他的纸。

一相认真地看了又看，很快就发现了他的纸。郭老爷又把先前胡桂的纸拿出来比较①，纸都是一样的。

郭老爷就问交纸的人

说：“你们的纸是从哪儿来的？”

这些人说：“我们的纸都是在城外谢惠(Xiè Huì)的店[1]里买的。”

① 店 (diàn) *n.* shop, store
e.g., 这里有很多商店，可以买到你想要的东西。

郭老爷让人把谢惠找来，问他："你这纸是从哪里来的？"

谢惠说："是一个叫竹（Zhú）青（Qīng）的人卖给我的。"

郭老爷马上让人骑[1]快马去把竹青带来。竹青来了，郭老爷问道：“竹青，是不是你抢了一相的纸？”

竹青说：“老爷，我去外地了，今天才回来。您怎么能说我抢了别人的纸呢？”

① 骑 (qí) *v.* ride
e.g., 你骑车的时候要小心一点。

郭老爷又问："那么这些纸是谁卖给谢惠的？"

竹青摇摇头，说："我真的不知道。"

谢惠在旁边说："前天早上，就是你把这些纸卖给了我。你怎么能说不知道呢？"

竹青看到谢惠，旁边还放着他抢来的纸，知道没办法了，只好说了真话："那天晚上，我看见有一只船停在河边，就找了几个朋友一起去抢船上的东西。船上有不少纸，我们下船的时候，有一个朋友不小心弄丢[1]了一些纸。第二天

① 弄丢 (nòngdiū)
lose
e.g., 你一定要小心，别把护照弄丢了。

早上，我就把剩下的纸卖给了谢惠。”

郭老爷听了，马上派人去把竹青的那些“朋友”抓了起来。一相的纸都找回来了，他非常感谢郭老爷。百姓们也都说，郭老爷这么快就找出了抢纸的坏人，真是个聪明的好官！

竹青和他的“朋友”们受到了严厉[1]的惩罚[2]，从那以后，广州很少再发生抢东西的事情。“审石头”的故事[3]也就流传[4]了下来。

① 严厉 (yánlì) *adj.*
stern, severe
e.g., 她的父亲非常严厉。

② 惩罚 (chéngfá) *v.*
punish
e.g., 他做错了事，受到了惩罚。

③ 故事 (gùshi) *n.*
story
e.g., 我很喜欢听故事。

④ 流传 (liúchuán) *v.*
hand down
e.g., 中国流传着很多有趣的神话故事。

English Version

A Stone on Trial

Many years ago, a man from Jiangxi Province named Yixiang rowed a boat to Guangzhou to sell paper because of the high price of paper there. He moored his boat at the riverbank and lived on it at night. One night, as he was about to fall asleep, he saw a lot of people charging onto his boat with torches and broadswords. They robbed him of his paper. Yixiang was terrified. He hid himself to stay out of their sights. The next morning, he reported the case to the local authorities.

The local official, whose surname was Guo, was quite smart. "Lord, I rowed a boat from Jiangxi to sell paper here," Yixiang told him, "but last night many bandits rushed onto my boat and stole all my paper. Can you help me retrieve it?"

"Did you see the bandits clearly?" Lord Guo asked.

"No, I didn't. It was very dark," Yixiang said.

"Then how can I help you? It will be too difficult!"

Hearing this, Yixiang became anxious and said, "I'm begging for your help. All the money I spent on the paper is borrowed. I can't return home if the paper cannot be retrieved. What should I do?"

Hearing this, Lord Guo said, "Don't worry. I will consider how to handle this case."

How could they capture the bandits? Lord Guo scratched his head and finally came up with a good solution. He dispatched four servants to find out if there was anyone who was selling paper.

When the four arrived at the gate of the town, they saw a person selling paper on one side of a street, whereupon they brought this person to Lord Guo.

"What is your name?" Lord Guo asked the seller.

"My name is Hu Gui," the seller said.

"Ask Yixiang to come to see if the paper sold by Hu Gui is his," Lord Guo said to the servants.

A moment later, Yixiang arrived. "Yixiang, is this your paper?" Lord Guo asked.

Yixiang inspected it again and again. "Yes, this is my paper!" he said. "Each piece of my paper is marked with a small character 相 (his name) at the bottom of the left side. Look! Each piece here has the character 相."

Lord Guo asked Hu Gui in a fury, "Why did you rob him of his paper?"

Hu Gui became worried. "Lord, I didn't steal his paper" he quickly said. "I have only an old mother in my family. My leg is not good, so it is difficult for me to walk. How would it be possible for me to rob someone?"

Lord Guo didn't think he was telling lies, so he went on to ask, "Where did you get the paper you sold? Can you clarify this?"

"This morning when I went to fetch water from the river," Hu

Gui said, "I saw a lot of paper lying along its bank and brought it back home. My mother told me that since we had been suffering from hunger for quite a few days, we might as well sell it and earn some money for meals. Lord, I really have no idea where the paper is from."

Hearing this, Lord Guo nodded his head. "I can't be sure if what you say is true," he said. "Servants, lock him up for now. Only when the real evildoer is captured should he be released."

Hearing this, Hu Gui burst into tears and said, "Lord, I'm fine to stay locked up here. But then my aged mother will be left at home alone. What should she do?"

After hearing this, Lord Guo smiled. "You are so filially pious," he said. "It is unlikely that you would do such a bad deed. You can go home first! But if I find out you stole the paper, I will not forgive you."

After Hu Gui left, Lord Guo began to consider how to capture the robbers. "Are there any objects near where you anchored your boat?" he asked Yixiang.

Yixiang thought for a while and said, "There is a big stone at the riverside."

"This stone must know who stole your paper," Lord Guo said in all seriousness. "Servants, go to the riverside and bring back that stone!" he shouted. "I will put it on trial and find out who stole Yixiang's paper." With this, he sent dozens of servants to the riverside to retrieve the big stone.

The servants put the stone in the middle of a big hall. Lord Guo began to interrogate it in all seriousness, "Stone, please immediately tell me who on earth stole Yixiang's paper."

All the servants laughed in a discreet manner and said, "Is our lord playing a joke? How can a stone speak?"

Quite quickly all the people knew there would be a trial of a stone conducted by Lord Guo. They were curious about it and came to see how Lord Guo could make a stone speak. Seeing so many people gathering around, Guo had his servants open the main gate and allowed them all to enter.

Lord Guo asked the stone seriously, "Stone, you must know who stole Yixiang's paper. Speak now!" Lord Guo asked three times, but the stone remained silent.

Lord Guo flew into a rage. "Servants, give the stone twenty heavy blows then see if it speaks or not," he shouted.

Seeing this, people burst into laughter.

"Why are you laughing?" Lord Guo said in fury. "Servants, close the gate; no one is allowed to leave!" When the gate was closed, those who had roared with laughter became a little frightened.

"How dare you laugh at me! How dare you look down upon me!" Lord Guo said. "In order to atone, do you consent to be fined or to be beaten with sticks?"

All the people said in unison, "We are willing to be fined."

"OK, write down your names and home addresses," Lord Guo said. "I will allow you to go home first, but each of you needs to hand over one hundred pieces of paper as punishment." Hearing this, they felt unhappy, but they had no choice but to do so.

Later that afternoon, everyone returned to the official residence and submitted the paper. Lord Guo asked Yixiang to see if his paper was among the pieces submitted.

Yixiang looked carefully and soon spotted his paper. Lord Guo then compared Hu Gui's paper with these pieces and found they were the same.

Lord Guo asked the people who submitted the paper, "Where did you buy your paper?"

"We bought it at Xie Hui's store outside the city," they said.

Lord Guo sent for Xie Hui and asked him, "Where is your paper from?"

"A man named Zhu Qing sold me the paper," Xie Hui said.

Lord Guo asked his servant to go by horseback and bring Zhu Qing to him quickly. As Zhu Qing arrived, Lord Guo asked, "Zhu Qing, did you steal Yixiang's paper?"

"Lord, I was out of town and just came back today," Zhu Qing said. "Why would you say I stole someone else's paper?"

Lord Guo asked again, "Who sold the paper to Xie Hui then?"

Zhu Qing shook his head and said, "I really have no idea."

Xie Hui then spoke up, "It was you who sold the paper to me on the morning of the day before yesterday. Why did you say you knew nothing about this? "

Seeing Xie Hui as well as the paper he had stolen, Zhu Qing had no choice but to tell the truth, "When I saw a boat moored at the riverside that night, I went to rob it together with several friends. There was a huge load of paper on board. When we got off, one person lost some paper due to carelessness, and the rest was sold to Xie Hui the next morning."

Hearing this, Lord Guo immediately dispatched the servants to arrest Zhu Qing's "friends". When they were captured, Yixiang's paper was retrieved. Yixiang showed a great appreciation to Lord Guo. The ordinary people acclaimed him as a resourceful official because he captured the thieves so quickly.

Zhu Qing and his "friends" were severely punished. Afterwards, robbery seldom took place in Guangzhou. Since then, the story of the trial of the stone has been handed down from generation to generation.

练习题 Reading exercises

一、选择题。 Choose the correct answer.

1. 一相的什么东西让人抢了？（　　）

A. 船　　B. 纸　　C. 石头　　D. 钱

2. 一相想去（　　）卖东西。

A. 江西　　B. 广州　　C. 北京　　D. 上海

3. 一相的纸上有个“(　　)”字。

A. 相　　B. 一　　C. 竹　　D. 青

4. (　　）抢了一相的纸？

A. 郭老爷　　B. 竹青　　C. 谢惠　　D. 胡桂

5. 人们为什么笑郭老爷？（　　）

A. 郭老爷审石头　　B. 郭老爷审胡桂

C. 郭老爷一本正经　　D. 郭老爷很认真

6. 胡桂在（　　）捡到了纸。

A. 船上　　B. 城里　　C. 店里　　D. 河边

7. (　　）把纸卖给了谢惠。

A. 胡桂　　B. 差人　　C. 竹青　　D. 一相

8. 郭老爷让人们交多少张纸当罚金？（　　）

A. 一百张　　B. 十张　　C. 五十张　　D. 五百张

9. 人们说郭老爷很（　　）。

A. 孝顺　　B. 严厉　　C. 聪明　　D. 一本正经

10. 大家都说郭老爷是个好官，因为（　　）。

A. 老百姓们告诉郭老爷谁抢了一相的纸

B. 石头告诉郭老爷谁抢了一相的纸

C. 他用审石头的方法找到了抢纸的人

D. 差人们抓到了抢一相纸的人

二、判断题：请根据故事内容判断下列说法是否正确，如果正确请标“T”，不正确请标“F”。

Decide whether the following statements are true (T) or false (F).

1. 一相划船去广州卖纸是因为那里的纸价格高。（　　）
2. 一相的纸都卖出去了。（　　）
3. 郭老爷审石头是为了找到抢纸的人。（　　）
4. 谢惠抢了一相的纸。（　　）
5. 胡桂家里有三个孩子。（　　）
6. 差人把官府大门关上的时候，大家都有一点儿害怕。（　　）
7. 人们都在交来的纸上写下了自己的名字和地址。（　　）

8. 竹青抢了谢惠的船。 (　　)

9. 谢惠是个很孝顺的儿子。 (　　)

10. 竹青和他的朋友们受到了严厉的惩罚。 (　　)

三、选择填空。 Choose the appropriate words to fill in the parentheses.

1. 很多年前，一相划（　　）去广州卖（　　）。有一天（　　），他把船停在河边，快要睡着的时候，突然有很多人冲到船上，（　　）走了他的纸，他非常（　　）。

A. 船　　B. 晚上　　C. 害怕　　D. 抢

E. 纸

2. 郭老爷让几个差人去把河边的（　　）抬来。他非常（　　），问石头："快（　　）！是谁抢了一相的纸？"可石头（　　）说话。看到郭老爷审石头，人们都（　　）了起来。

A. 说　　B. 石头　　C. 生气　　D. 笑

E. 不会

四、连线题。 Match.

1. 请把下列人物和事件搭配起来。

A. 郭老爷	a. 抢走了别人的纸
B. 竹青	b. 让人们交纸充当罚金
C. 一相	c. 买了一相被抢的纸
D. 谢惠	d. 纸被抢了，去官府告状
E. 差人	e. 骑马抓坏人

2. 请为下列词语选择合适的搭配。

A. 交	a. 石头
B. 受	b. 惩罚
C. 抬	c. 吃的
D. 买	d. 罚金

五、请根据故事内容给下列句子排列顺序。
Put the following statements in order according to the story.

A. 郭老爷审石头。

B. 城里的人们跑来看郭老爷审石头，大家都笑他。

C. 一相的纸被人抢走了。

D. 一相去官府找郭老爷告状。

E. 郭老爷让大家写下名字、地址，回家拿一百张纸来。

F. 郭老爷关了门，不让大家出去。

G. 一相从里面找到了自己的纸。

六、图片题。 Answer the following questions according to the picture.

1. 请根据故事内容，说说这幅图应该放在这本书的（　　）页。

2. 图片中都有哪些人物？

3. 图中的人物在做什么？

4. 他们的表情有什么不一样？

5. 请你用中文或英文给这幅图加一个简单的标题说明。

练习题答案 Keys to the exercises

一、选择题

1. B　　2. B　　3. A　　4. B　　5. A
6. D　　7. C　　8. A　　9. C　　10. C

二、判断题：请根据故事内容判断下列说法是否正确，如果正确请标“T”，不正确请标“F”

1. T　　2. F　　3. T　　4. F　　5. F
6. T　　7. F　　8. F　　9. F　　10. T

三、选择填空

1. A　　E　　B　　D　　C
2. B　　C　　A　　E　　D

四、连线题

1. A-b, B-a, C-d, D-c, E-e　　2. A-d, B-b, C-a, D-c

五、请根据故事内容给下列句子排列顺序

C-D-A-B-F-E-G

六、略。

词汇表
Vocabulary List

挨打		ái dǎ	suffer from beating
办法	*n.*	bànfǎ	method, solution
饱	*adj.*	bǎo	full, replete
报案	*v.*	bào àn	report a case
比较	*v.*	bǐjiào	compare
差人	*n.*	chāirén	bailiff, runner
惩罚	*v.*	chéngfá	punish
聪明	*adj.*	cōngmíng	smart, intelligent
大厅	*n.*	dàtīng	hall
带	*v.*	dài	take, bring
刀	*n.*	dāo	knife, sword
地址	*n.*	dìzhǐ	address
店	*n.*	diàn	shop, store
躲	*v.*	duǒ	hide
罚金	*n.*	fájīn	fine, forfeit
敢	*v.*	gǎn	dare
故事	*n.*	gùshi	story
官府	*n.*	guānfǔ	administrative body
害怕	*adj.*	hàipà	scared, frightened
好奇	*adj.*	hàoqí	curious
河	*n.*	hé	river
划船	*v.*	huá chuán	row (a boat)
火把	*n.*	huǒbǎ	torch
价格	*n.*	jiàgé	price
交	*v.*	jiāo	hand over, submit
老爷	*n.*	lǎoye	lord, master
流传	*v.*	liúchuán	hand down
弄丢		nòngdiū	lose
骑	*v.*	qí	ride
抢	*v.*	qiǎng	rob, loot, scramble for
清楚	*adj.*	qīngchu	clear
审	*v.*	shěn	try, interrogate

石头	*n.*	shítou	stone
抬	*v.*	tái	carry, move
停	*v.*	tíng	park, berth
偷偷	*adv.*	tōutōu	stealthily, on the sly
腿	*n.*	tuǐ	leg
孝顺	*v.*	xiàoshùn	show filial piety
严厉	*adj.*	yánlì	stern, severe
一本正经		yìběn-zhèngjīng	in all seriousness
纸	*n.*	zhǐ	paper
抓	*v.*	zhuā	capture

项目策划：韩　颖　刘小琳
责任编辑：韩　颖
英文编辑：薛彧威
英文审定：黄长奇　James Hutchison
设计指导：战文庭　卞　淳
设计制作：isles studio

图书在版编目（CIP）数据

审石头 / 宋晶改编. -- 北京 : 华语教学出版社, 2018.7
（“彩虹桥”汉语分级读物. 1级 : 300词）
ISBN 978-7-5138-1478-2

Ⅰ. ①审… Ⅱ. ①宋… Ⅲ. ①汉语—对外汉语教学—语言读物 Ⅳ. ①H195.5

中国版本图书馆CIP数据核字（2017）第313355号

审石头
宋　晶　改编
吴爱俊　翻译
*

华语教学出版社有限责任公司出版
（中国北京百万庄大街24号　邮政编码 100037）
电话：(86)10-68320585　68997826
传真：(86)10-68997826　68326333
网址：www.sinolingua.com.cn
电子信箱：hyjx@sinolingua.com.cn
北京京华虎彩印刷有限公司印刷
2018年（32开）第1版
2018年第1版第1次印刷
（汉英）
ISBN 978-7-5138-1478-2
定价：15.00元